Their Great Gift

Their Great Gift

COURAGE, SACRIFICE, and HOPE in a NEW LAND

John Coy PHOTOGRAPHS BY **Wing Young Huie**

because they dreamed of more.

Their journey was long and difficult,

and when they arrived,

they didn't know the language
or how to do certain things.

They made mistakes and people laughed.

Others didn't understand how much they'd sacrificed.

They worked long, hard hours, at difficult jobs.

They got up early, stayed late,

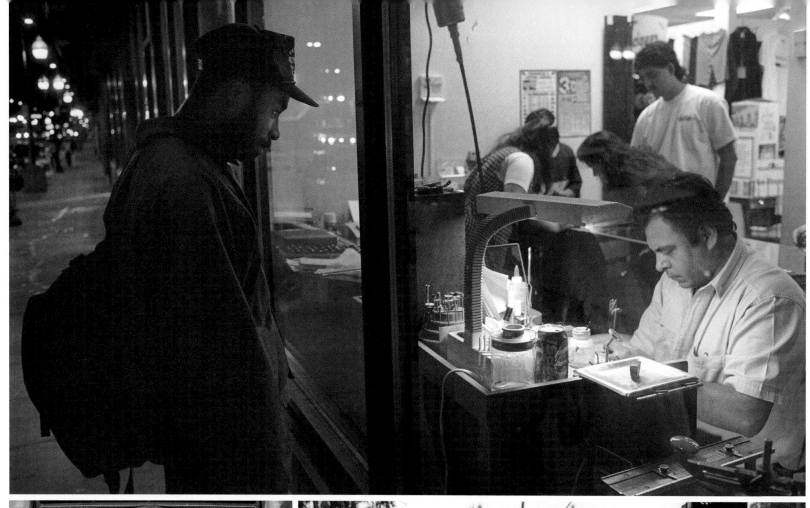

and took the extra shift.

They saved and did without

and sent money back.

They opened businesses

and poured all that they had into them.

They shifted between languages,

between cultures,

between places.

They gave advice:

"Work hard."

"Do well in school."

"Never give up."

They kept going day after day

so we'd have choices they didn't have.

And now, we're all here together

with our own arrival stories,

but one question keeps rising:

What will we do
with THEIR GREAT GIFT?

My ancestors came from Poland, Bavaria, Ireland, and Scotland. I chose this photograph to share because it includes the grandma I knew best. Mathilda Friedl, the youngest girl in the photo, received her name after an older sister with that name died from scarlet fever at the age of seven. My grandmother, who was born in 1896, was called Little Tillie to distinguish her from her dead sister Big Tillie. The other children are Rose, Max, and Mary. Mary later died in an influenza epidemic.

The parents, Joseph Friedl and Mathilda Fischer, grew up fourteen miles apart in Bavaria, but they did not know each other there.

They met in Saint Paul, Minnesota, where they had arrived and were working. After marrying and saving enough money, they bought a farm outside Albany, Minnesota. My grandma, as the youngest child, was permitted to read while her brother and sisters did chores.

Because she loved reading, she did well in school and became a teacher. Starting at sixteen, she taught in a one-room schoolhouse where some of the students were bigger than she was. With my grandfather Joseph Kulas, she had seven children, three of whom died as babies. She raised the four others on her own for many years while my grandfather was away in a tuberculosis sanatorium.

Through all of this, my grandmother passed on her love of reading and writing. Her four children all graduated from college, including my mother, Luanne Kulas Coy, who became the first woman in the family to do so.

My grandma lived to the age of ninety-three, and she paved the way for me.

—John Coy

time, owned a Chinese American restaurant. Joe Huie's Café served chop suey and egg foo young as well as pot roast and chicken-fried steak. For many years the restaurant was open every day, twenty-four hours, and my father, Joe, seldom took a day off, working from eight in the morning to eight at night.

I started working in the family business when I was twelve. My first job was to keep the books, carefully writing down in longhand the restaurant's expenses in a ledger. I then became a cashier, waiter, and cook. I would tearfully complain that none of my friends had to work, but in retrospect, I had it much easier than my oldest brothers, who had to be at the restaurant every single day, long weekends and school days, while I mostly worked in the summer.

My mother was a stay-at-home mom, raising me and my siblings, taking care of our tiny brick house, tending the garden in back, and constantly writing letters to relatives back in China. My father finally closed the restaurant and retired when I was a junior in high school. Several years later, in college, I bought a Minolta SLR camera. Mom and Dad became my first photography subjects.

—Wing Young Huie

I am the youngest of six children and the only one in my family not born in Guangzhou, China (two of my brothers are missing from this family photo, taken when I was about four). My parents, my four brothers, and my sister left China at different times in the early and mid 1900s, part of what is called the first and second wave of Chinese immigration to America.

I, however, was born and raised in Duluth, Minnesota. Our family, typical of Chinese at the

ARRIVING AT A BOOK

Books don't come out of nowhere. They are born from observations, conversations, research, school visits and, sometimes, from basketball.

As John says, "Wing and I first met each other twenty-five years ago playing basketball and became friends through spending hundreds of hours on the court. When editor Andrew Karre told me that he'd love to do a book with Wing, I leapt at the chance. I'd always wanted to write about my family's arrival stories and had been researching them for years. I knew of Wing's interest in immigration and had seen many of his striking photographs. I wrote text that was revised many times as we decided on pictures. While every family's arrival story is distinct, I wanted to focus on the overarching connections between immigrants—and between us all. Designers Danielle Carnito and Zach Marell, editor Carol Hinz, and project consultant Stephanie L. Rogers provided invaluable guidance long the way."

Wing did not take photographs specifically for this book, but he has been exploring the immigrant experience for most of his life. As he says, "These photographs are from thirty years of my career, showing everyday life in neighborhoods. Many were taken in my home state of Minnesota, but some are from different regions throughout the United States. The people shown have emigrated from many countries, including Mexico, Laos, Somalia, China, Sweden, Haiti, Latvia, Korea, and Nigeria. I searched through my extensive archive to select the people and families whose lives embodied the stories in *Their Great Gift*. John was gracious to allow me to make suggestions in his text that reflect what I've learned about the many immigrant experiences, and he gave me feedback about the photographs. As in basketball, we assisted each other along the way."